(1) **Copyright © 2021 by Doctor Melody**

(2) All rights reserved. No part of this book may be reproduced or used in any manner without written permission of the copyright owner except for the use of quotations in a book review.

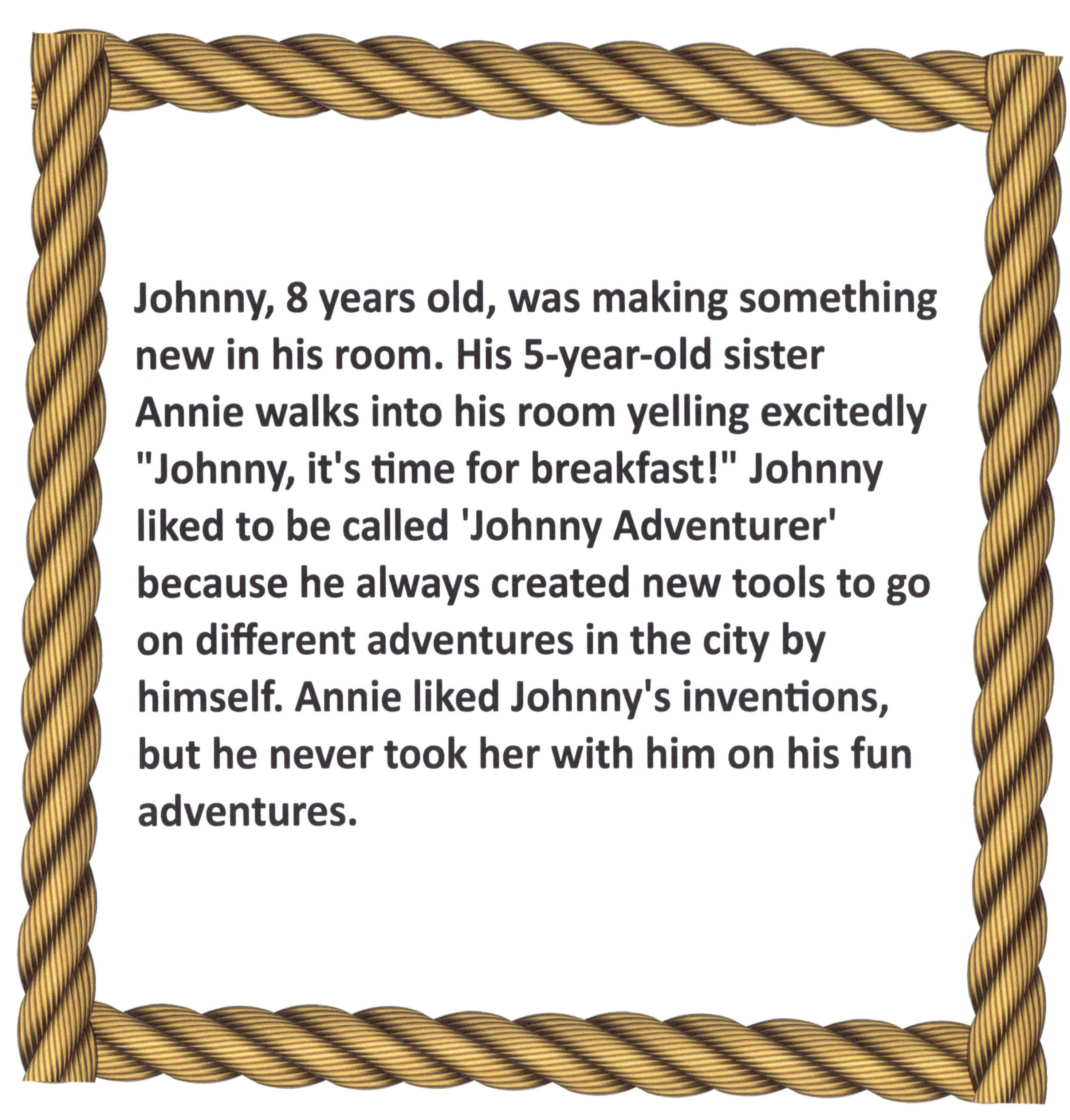

Johnny, 8 years old, was making something new in his room. His 5-year-old sister Annie walks into his room yelling excitedly "Johnny, it's time for breakfast!" Johnny liked to be called 'Johnny Adventurer' because he always created new tools to go on different adventures in the city by himself. Annie liked Johnny's inventions, but he never took her with him on his fun adventures.

1

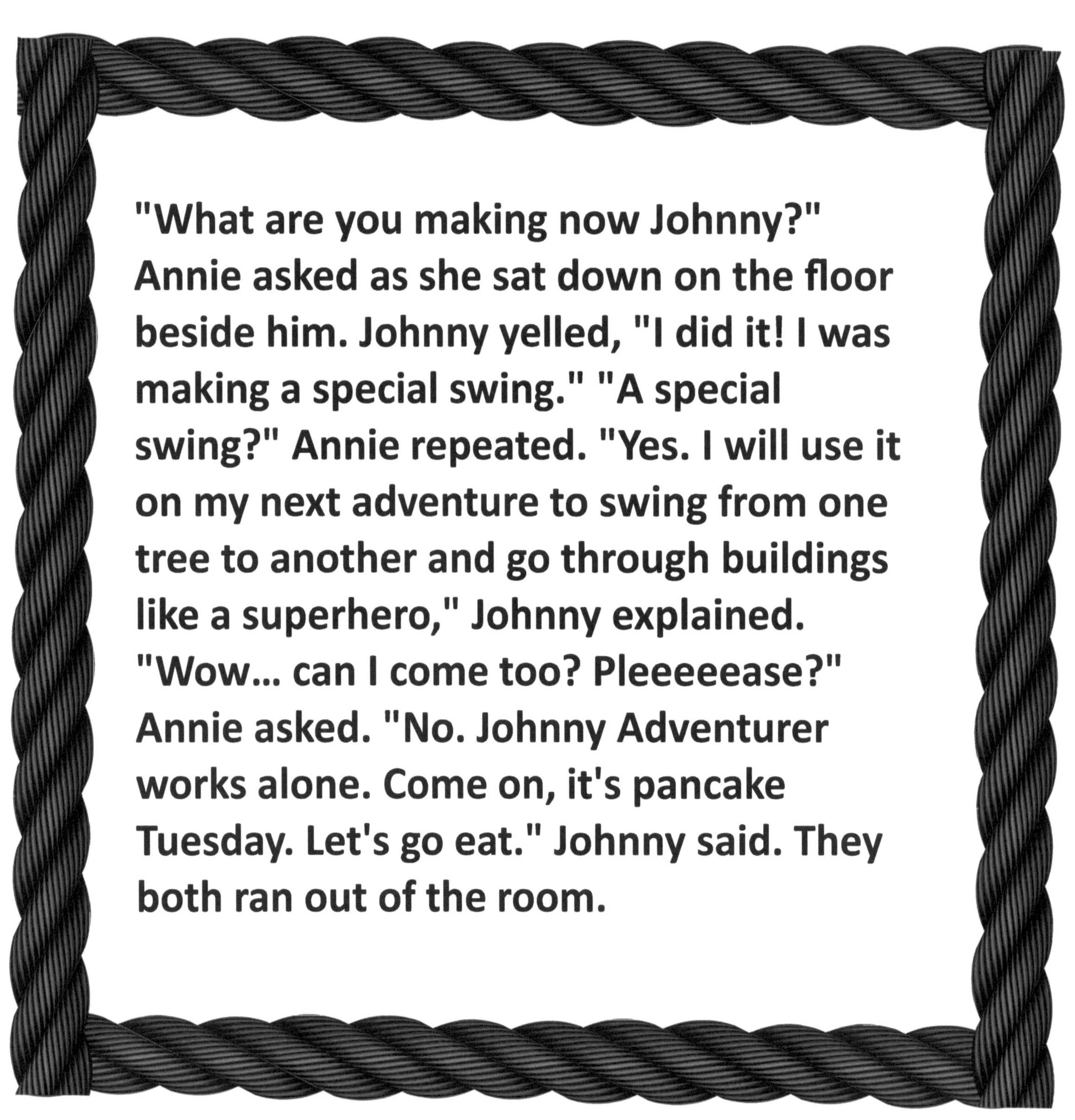

"What are you making now Johnny?" Annie asked as she sat down on the floor beside him. Johnny yelled, "I did it! I was making a special swing." "A special swing?" Annie repeated. "Yes. I will use it on my next adventure to swing from one tree to another and go through buildings like a superhero," Johnny explained. "Wow... can I come too? Pleeeeease?" Annie asked. "No. Johnny Adventurer works alone. Come on, it's pancake Tuesday. Let's go eat." Johnny said. They both ran out of the room.

2

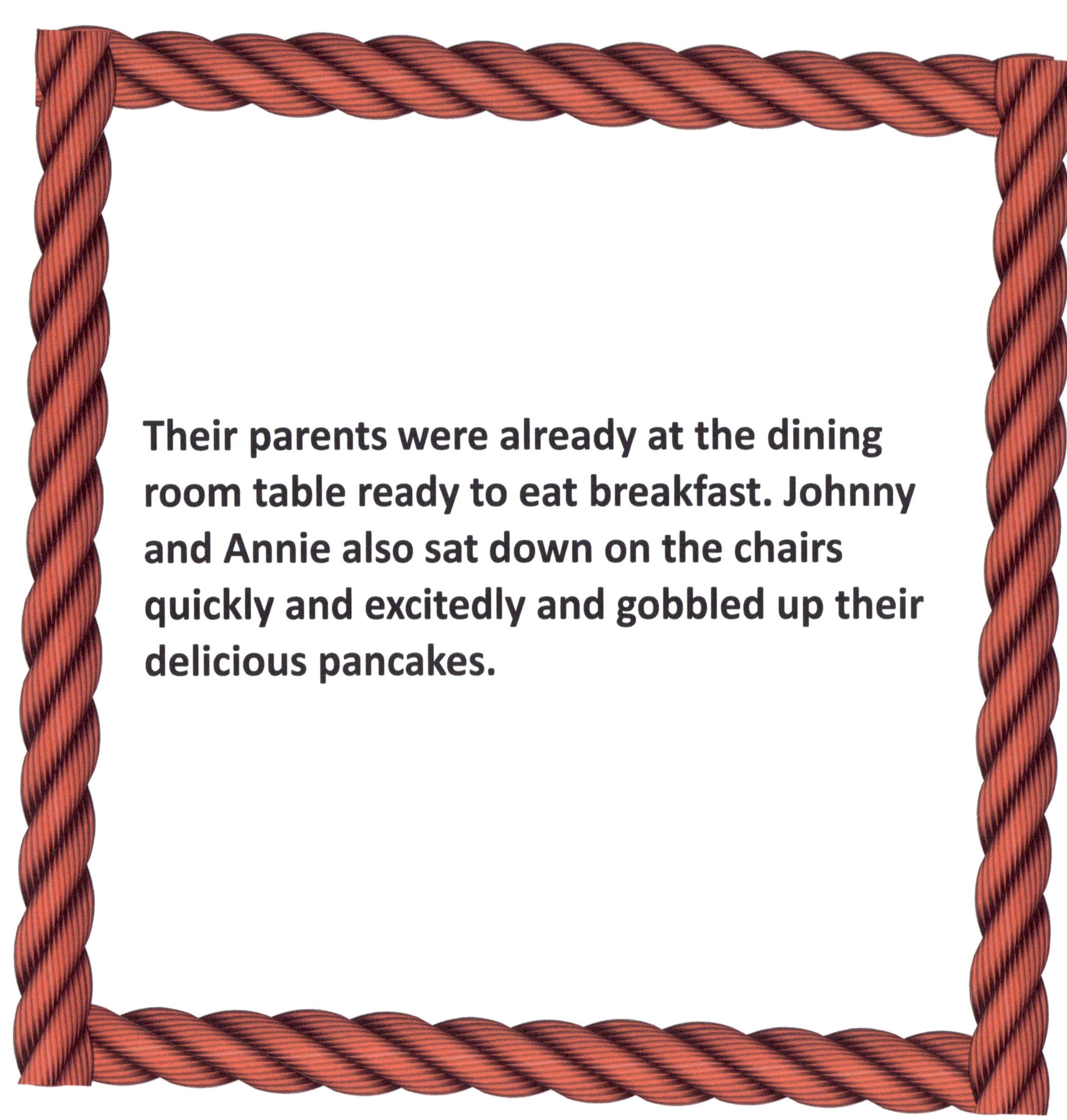

Their parents were already at the dining room table ready to eat breakfast. Johnny and Annie also sat down on the chairs quickly and excitedly and gobbled up their delicious pancakes.

3

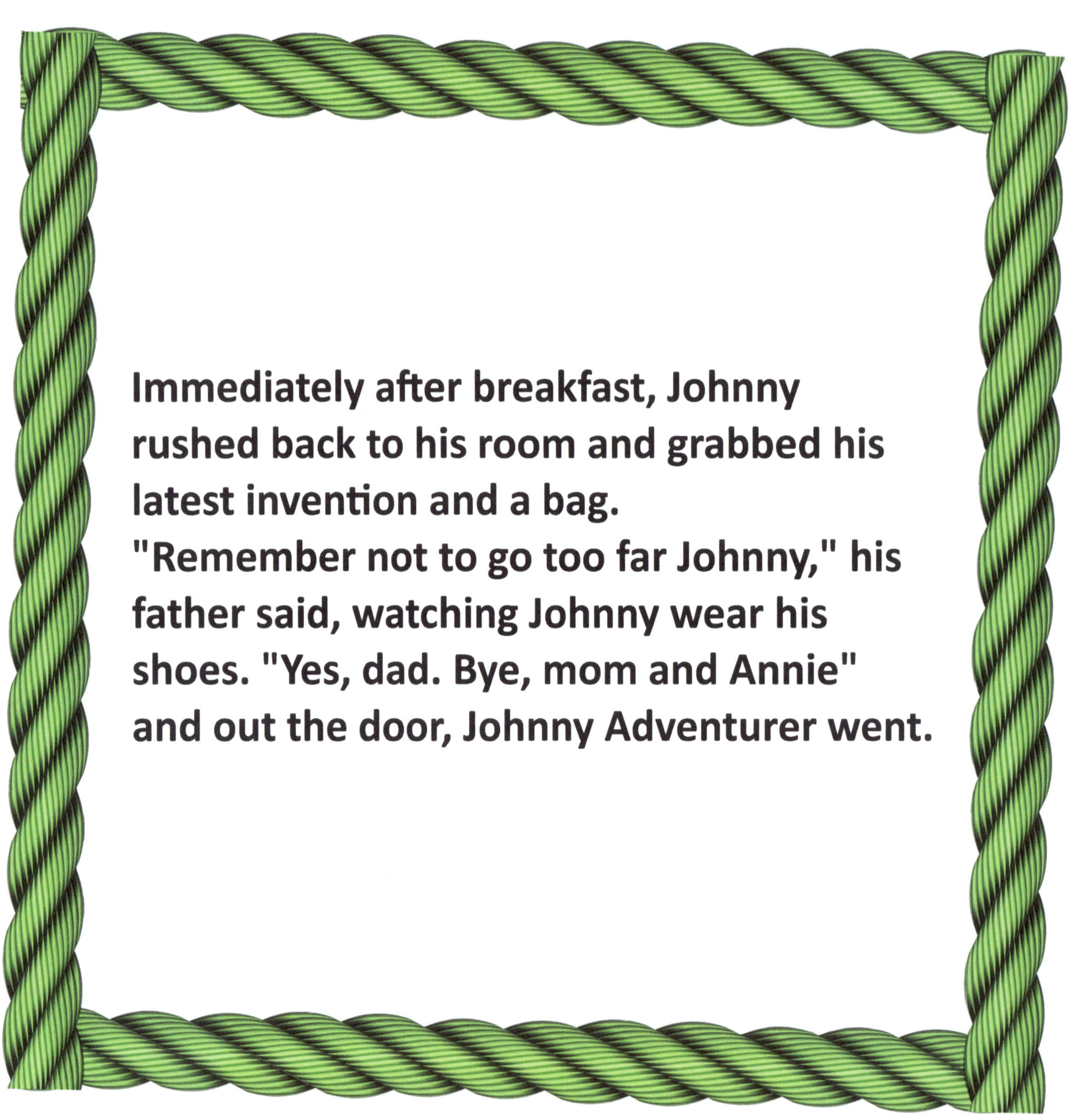

Immediately after breakfast, Johnny
rushed back to his room and grabbed his
latest invention and a bag.
"Remember not to go too far Johnny," his
father said, watching Johnny wear his
shoes. "Yes, dad. Bye, mom and Annie"
and out the door, Johnny Adventurer went.

4

Johnny decided that Rock Square Park was the best place to have an adventure today because it was close to his house so he walked there. He wanted to test his special swing in the trees. There were other kids playing around in the park. Johnny found a good spot with no kids to start his adventure. "First, I will survey the area with my super far sight," Johnny said. He pulled out his binoculars from his bag to look through it. "All seems clear. Now to swing through the trees!" he announced. Johnny pulled out his latest invention, which was a toy crossbow with a rope and a plunger attached to it.

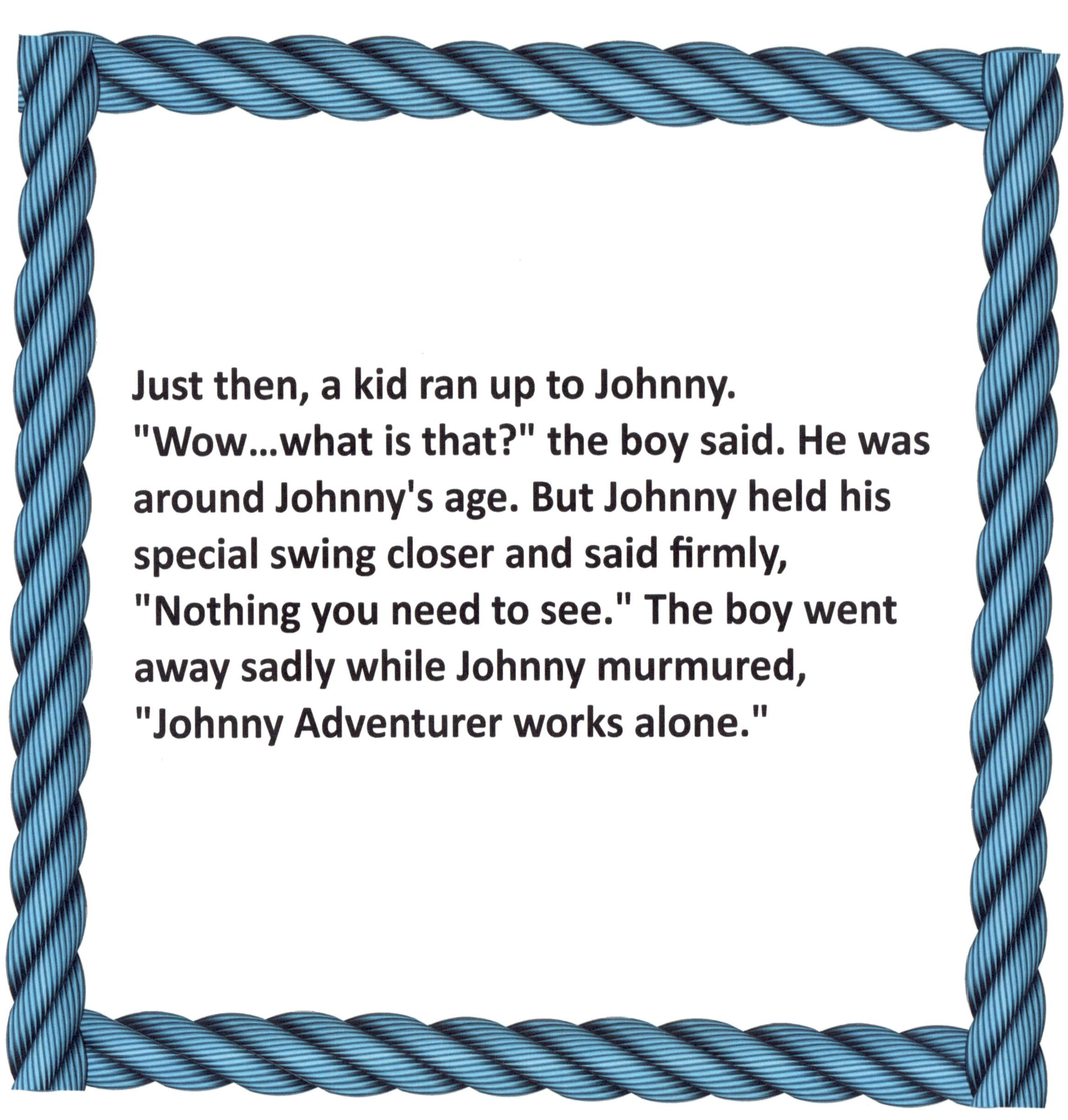

Just then, a kid ran up to Johnny. "Wow…what is that?" the boy said. He was around Johnny's age. But Johnny held his special swing closer and said firmly, "Nothing you need to see." The boy went away sadly while Johnny murmured, "Johnny Adventurer works alone."

6

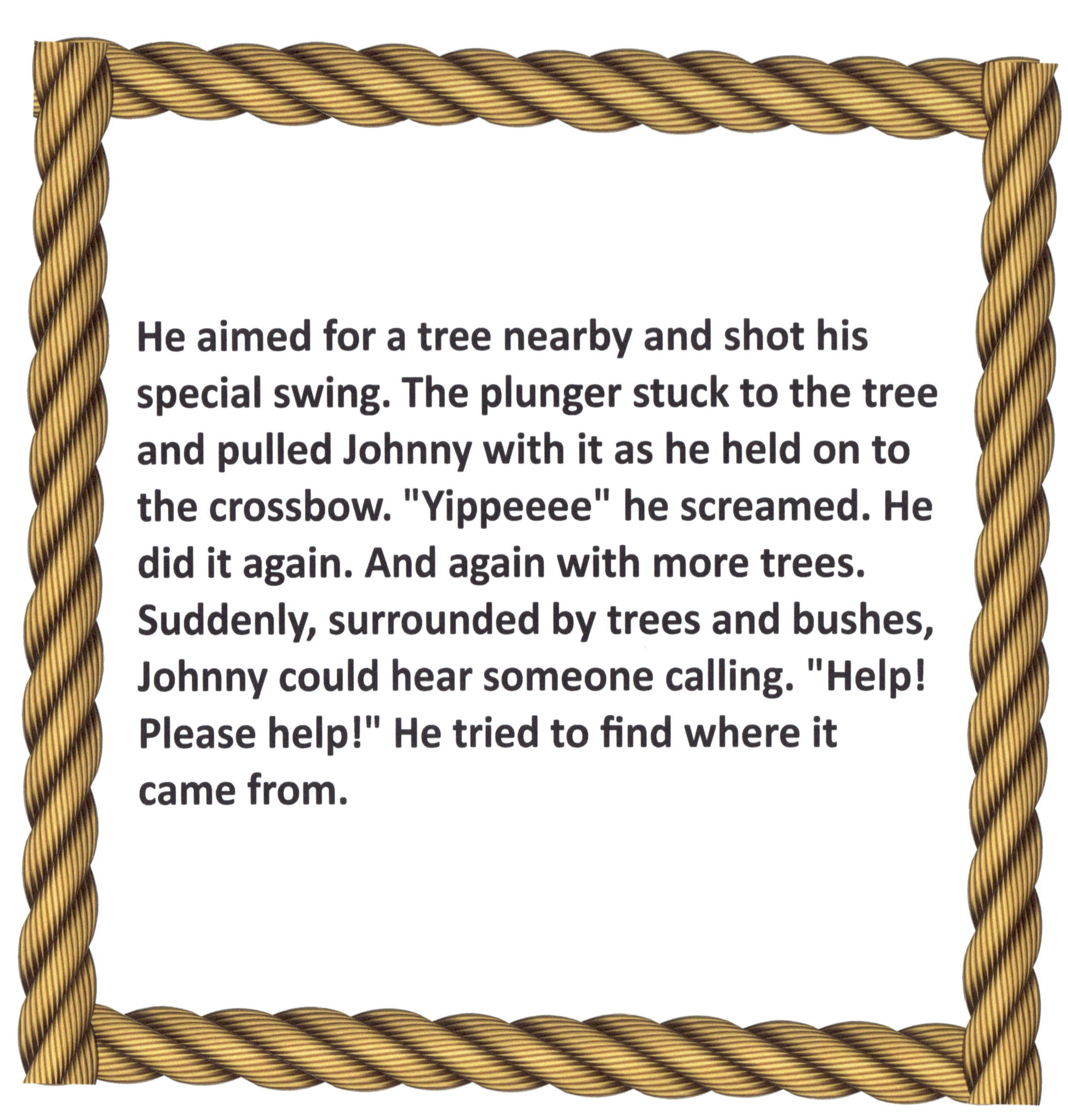

He aimed for a tree nearby and shot his special swing. The plunger stuck to the tree and pulled Johnny with it as he held on to the crossbow. "Yippeeee" he screamed. He did it again. And again with more trees. Suddenly, surrounded by trees and bushes, Johnny could hear someone calling. "Help! Please help!" He tried to find where it came from.

7

Johnny saw a little squirrel trapped in a net hanging from a tree. "A squirrel? How did you get trapped in there?" Johnny asked. "I don't know. I was scurrying through the trees when the net caught me. Please help me get out." The squirrel begged., "No, Johnny Adventurer does not help strangers." Johnny said. "Please help me, Johnny Adventurer." Said the squirrel. Johnny stopped in his tracks hearing his favorite name." All right, I'll help you" he said. Johnny aimed for the branch of the tree and shot his special swing. He held on to the tree as he grabbed the net. When he climbed down, he released the squirrel from the net. The squirrel was so happy.

8

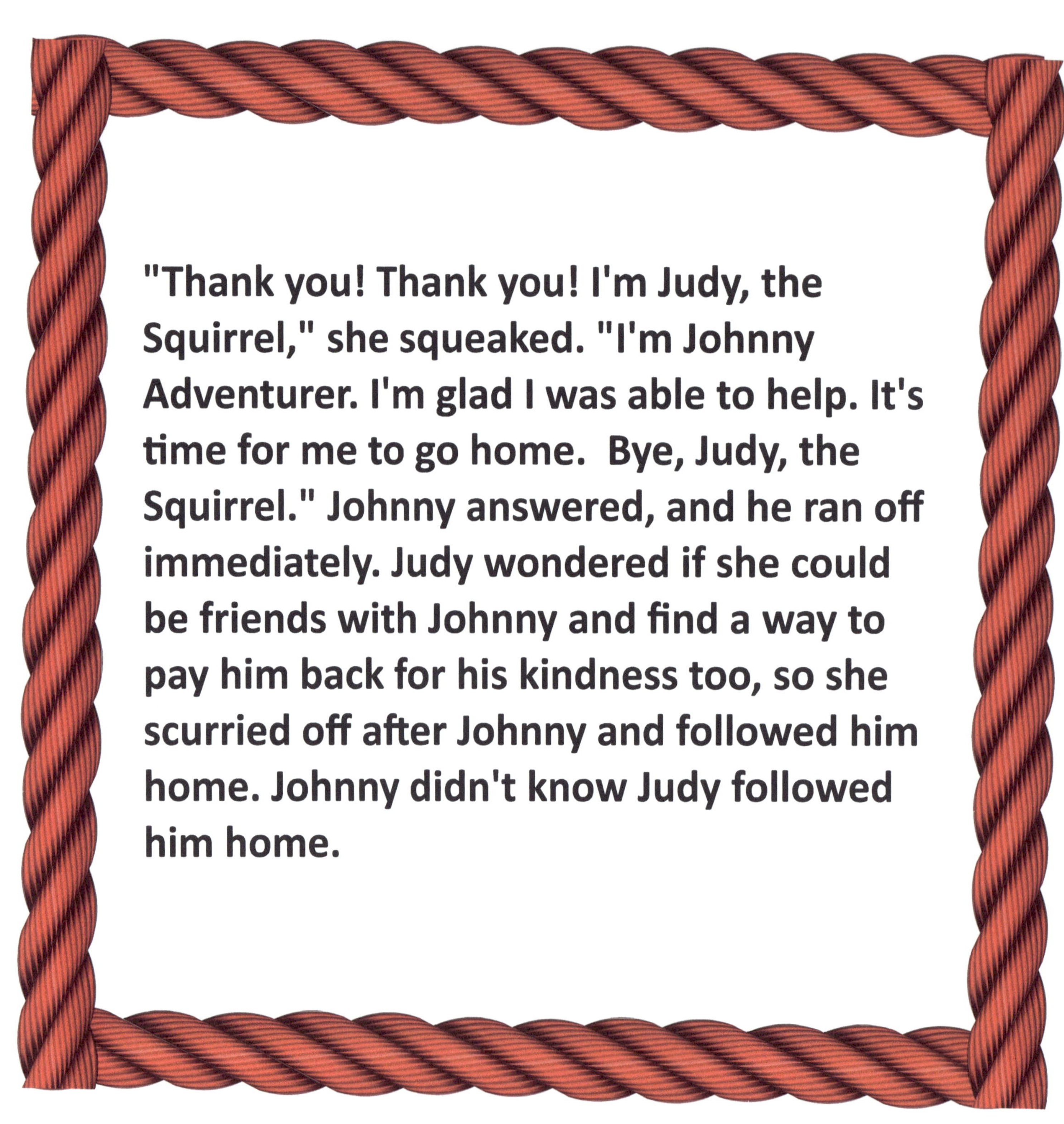

"Thank you! Thank you! I'm Judy, the Squirrel," she squeaked. "I'm Johnny Adventurer. I'm glad I was able to help. It's time for me to go home. Bye, Judy, the Squirrel." Johnny answered, and he ran off immediately. Judy wondered if she could be friends with Johnny and find a way to pay him back for his kindness too, so she scurried off after Johnny and followed him home. Johnny didn't know Judy followed him home.

9

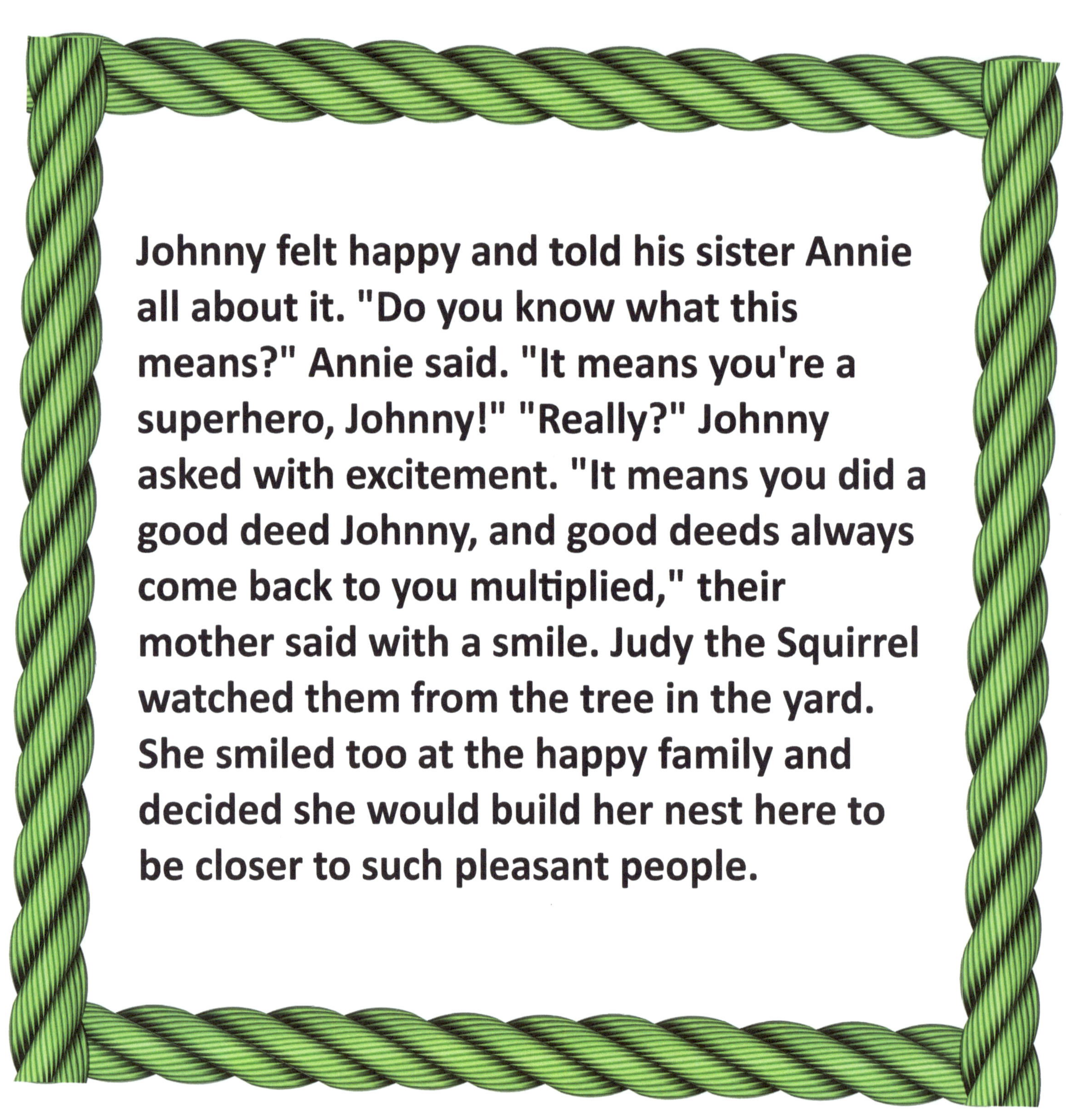

Johnny felt happy and told his sister Annie all about it. "Do you know what this means?" Annie said. "It means you're a superhero, Johnny!" "Really?" Johnny asked with excitement. "It means you did a good deed Johnny, and good deeds always come back to you multiplied," their mother said with a smile. Judy the Squirrel watched them from the tree in the yard. She smiled too at the happy family and decided she would build her nest here to be closer to such pleasant people.

10

One night, Judy saw smoke and fire in the kitchen through the window. The fire and smoke were going to spread and Johnny and his family were fast asleep. She had to warn them. Judy the Squirrel tried banging against the front door of the house. No one heard her. She climbed up to Johnny's bedroom window and made more noise banging on the window. The smoke had already spread to the bedroom. Then she hopped down to the yard and searched desperately for something to use. She found a rock she could carry and she climbed up to the outside of Johnny's bedroom and hurled it at the window. She smashed the window and hopped in. Judy jumped on Johnny's face and started hitting him with her small hands. Luckily, Johnny woke up just in time to see Judy and the smoke in the room.

11

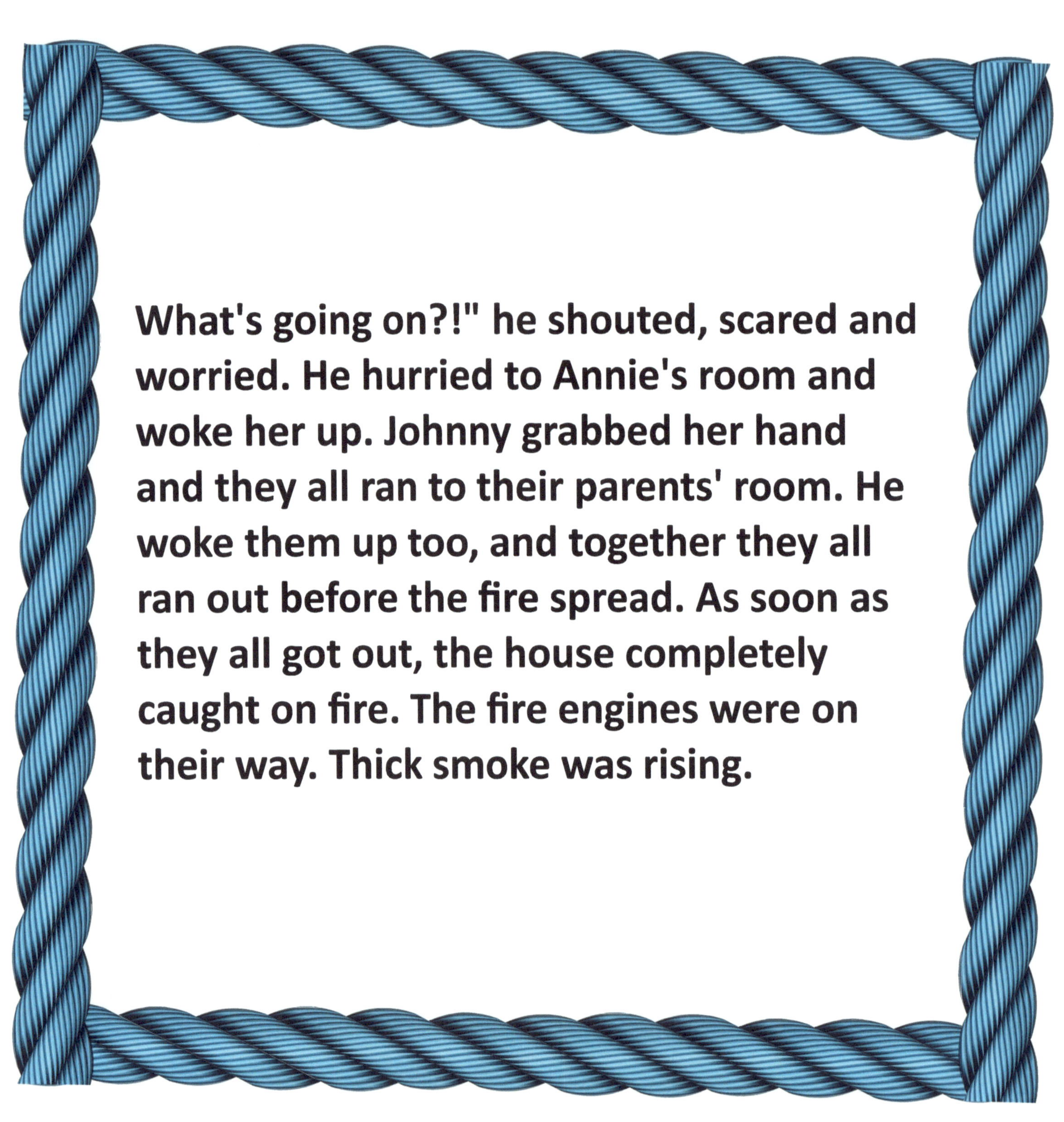

What's going on?!" he shouted, scared and worried. He hurried to Annie's room and woke her up. Johnny grabbed her hand and they all ran to their parents' room. He woke them up too, and together they all ran out before the fire spread. As soon as they all got out, the house completely caught on fire. The fire engines were on their way. Thick smoke was rising.

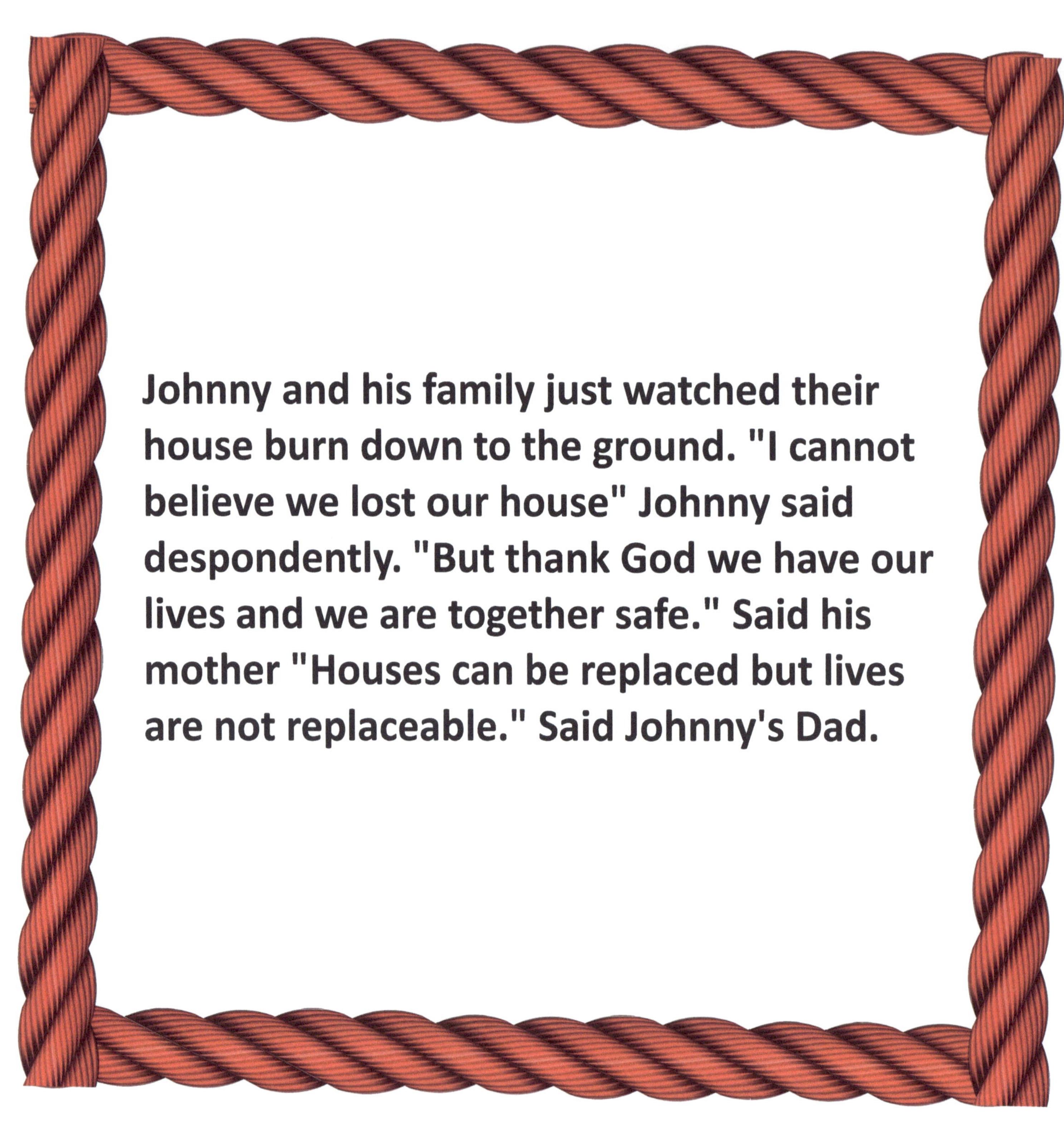

Johnny and his family just watched their house burn down to the ground. "I cannot believe we lost our house" Johnny said despondently. "But thank God we have our lives and we are together safe." Said his mother "Houses can be replaced but lives are not replaceable." Said Johnny's Dad.

13

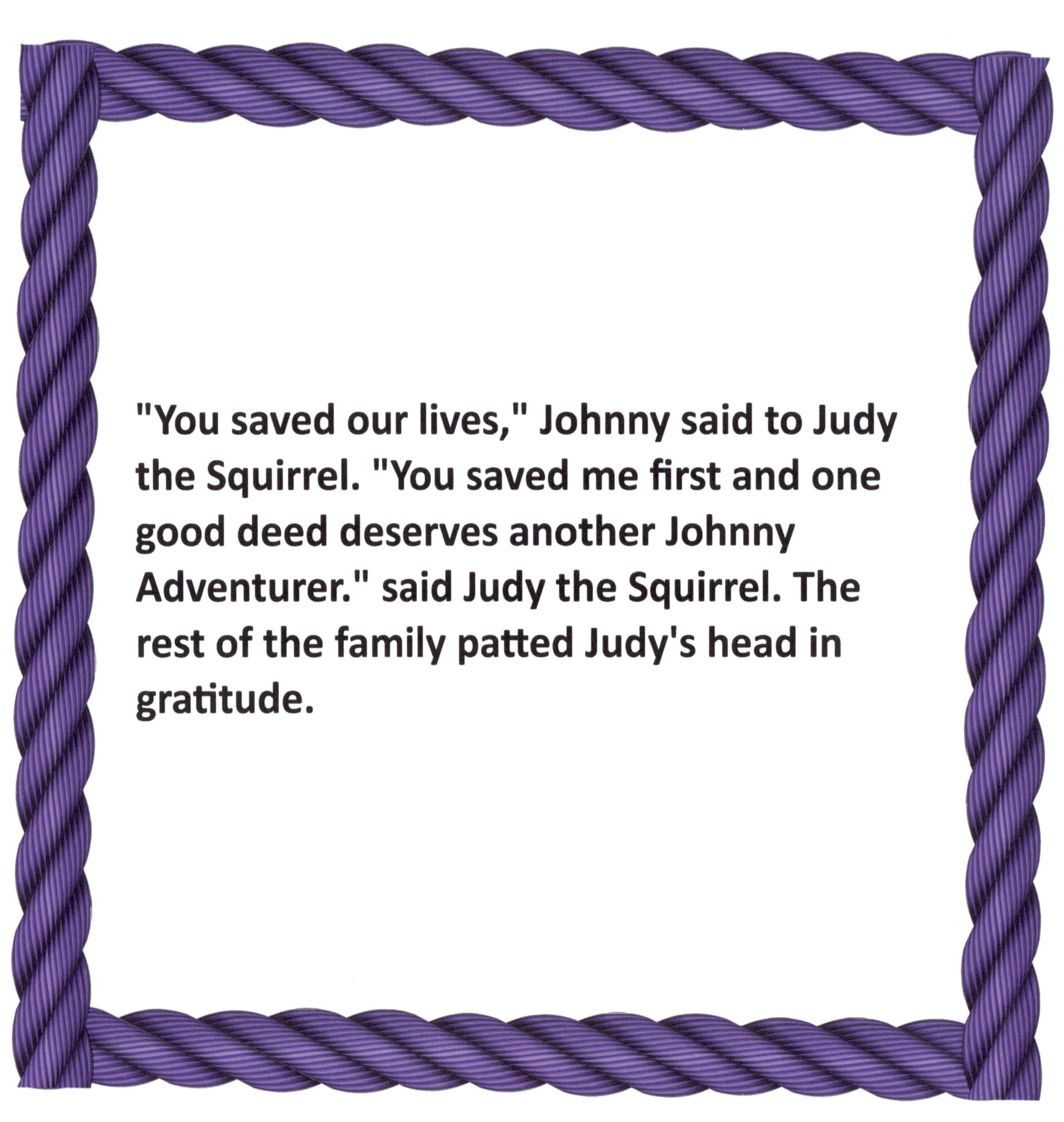

"You saved our lives," Johnny said to Judy the Squirrel. "You saved me first and one good deed deserves another Johnny Adventurer." said Judy the Squirrel. The rest of the family patted Judy's head in gratitude.

14

www.ingramcontent.com/pod-product-compliance
Lightning Source LLC
Chambersburg PA
CBHW042122110726
48006CB00003B/729